WHO WHO ARE YOU?

Cornelius Goes to Church

*For our beloved grandsons Λεωνίδας & Πίλιππε ♥
Με΄αγάπη,
Παππού & Γιαγιά
2024*

Written & Illustrated by Christina Herron

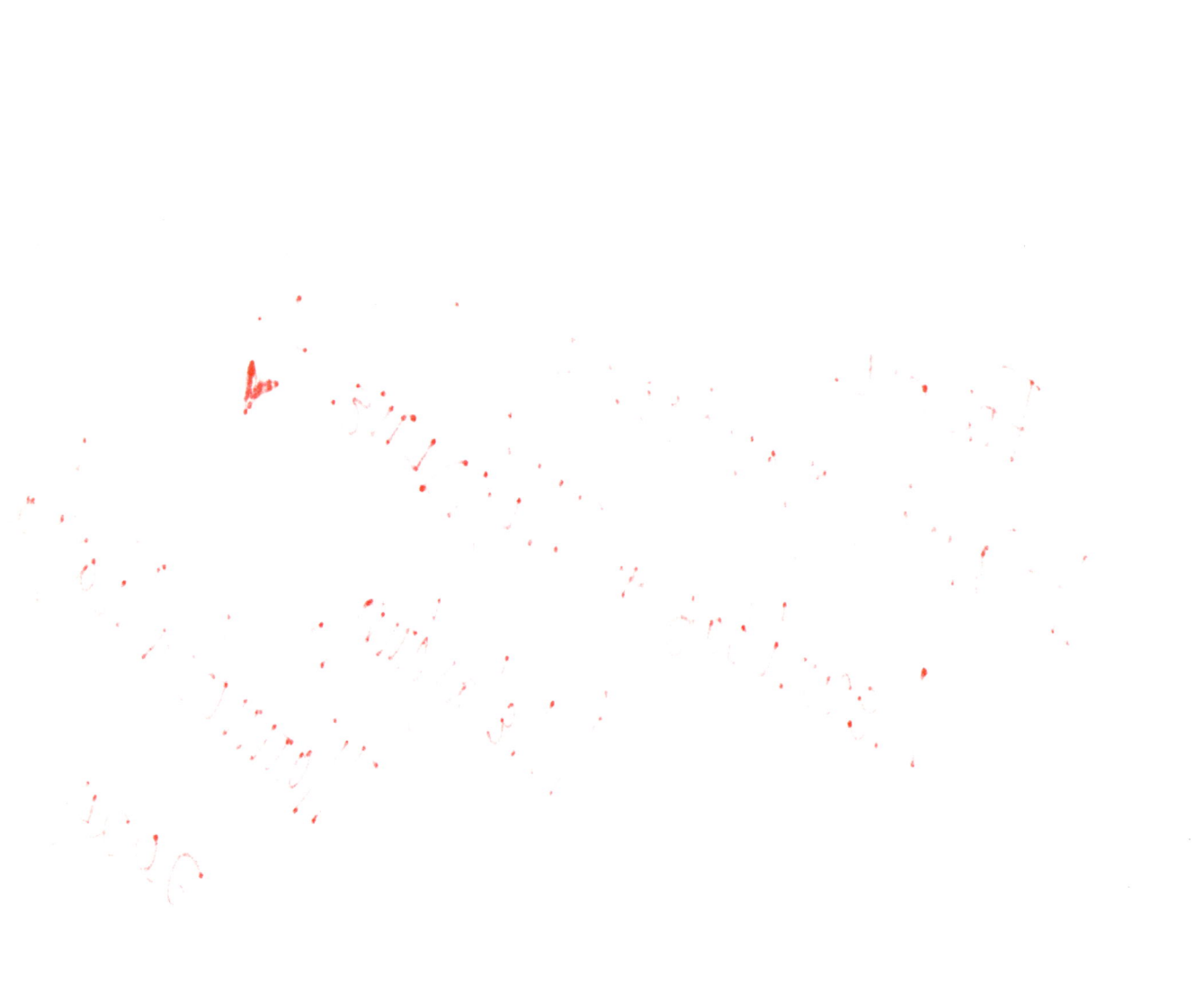

May you find as much joy in this story
as I found creating it. God Bless you
in all your endeavors.

One bright Sunday morning from up in his tree,
Cornelius, the owl, looked out to see
A beautiful church adorned with a cross,
But what it was for, he was at a loss.

I wonder, he thought, what this place is about.
What goes on inside there I must find out!

When all of a sudden, a man in all black
Passed under the tree with a rather large stack
Of books and gold vestments, some bread, and some wine.
Making his way to the church right on time.

WHO, WHO ARE YOU? Cornelius said,
And where are you going with that wine and bread?

I am the priest. I lead people in prayer.
I prepare communion for God's children to share.
I preach and I teach about Christ and the gospels,
About saints and the lives of the holy apostles.

I bless the people again and again
In the name of the Father, Son, Holy Spirit, Amen.

Thanks for explaining, Cornelius replied
And with that, the priest went on inside.

Soon after the priest went into the church,
Cornelius saw something from up in his perch,
A man in a long black robe appeared
With stacks of music and a long flowing beard

WHO WHO ARE YOU? Cornelius asked.
Where are you off to walking so fast?

I am the chanter, I lead people in song
Praying the hymns of the church short and long.
I have learned all of the tones, many prayers and the Psalms,
The words of the Church Fathers I chant in songs.

I reply 'Lord, Have Mercy' when the priest prays again and again.
Grant this, O Lord, Alleluia, Amen.

Thanks for explaining, Cornelius replied.
And with that, the chanter went on inside.

Just a few minutes later, a young boy ran past.
WHO WHO ARE YOU? Cornelius asked.
Why are you carrying a gold robe and a book?
And is that a candle? Can I take a look?

'Oh, hello, Mr. Owl!' the little boy stated.
He showed him his items and was quite elated.
This is my robe, I serve in the altar.
I stand up very straight and try never to falter

I hold my candle while the Gospel is read
And I help cut the Antidoron bread.
I prepare the censor with nice smelling incense,
That carries our prayers up to God's presence.

Thanks for explaining, Cornelius replied
And with that, the altar boy went on inside.

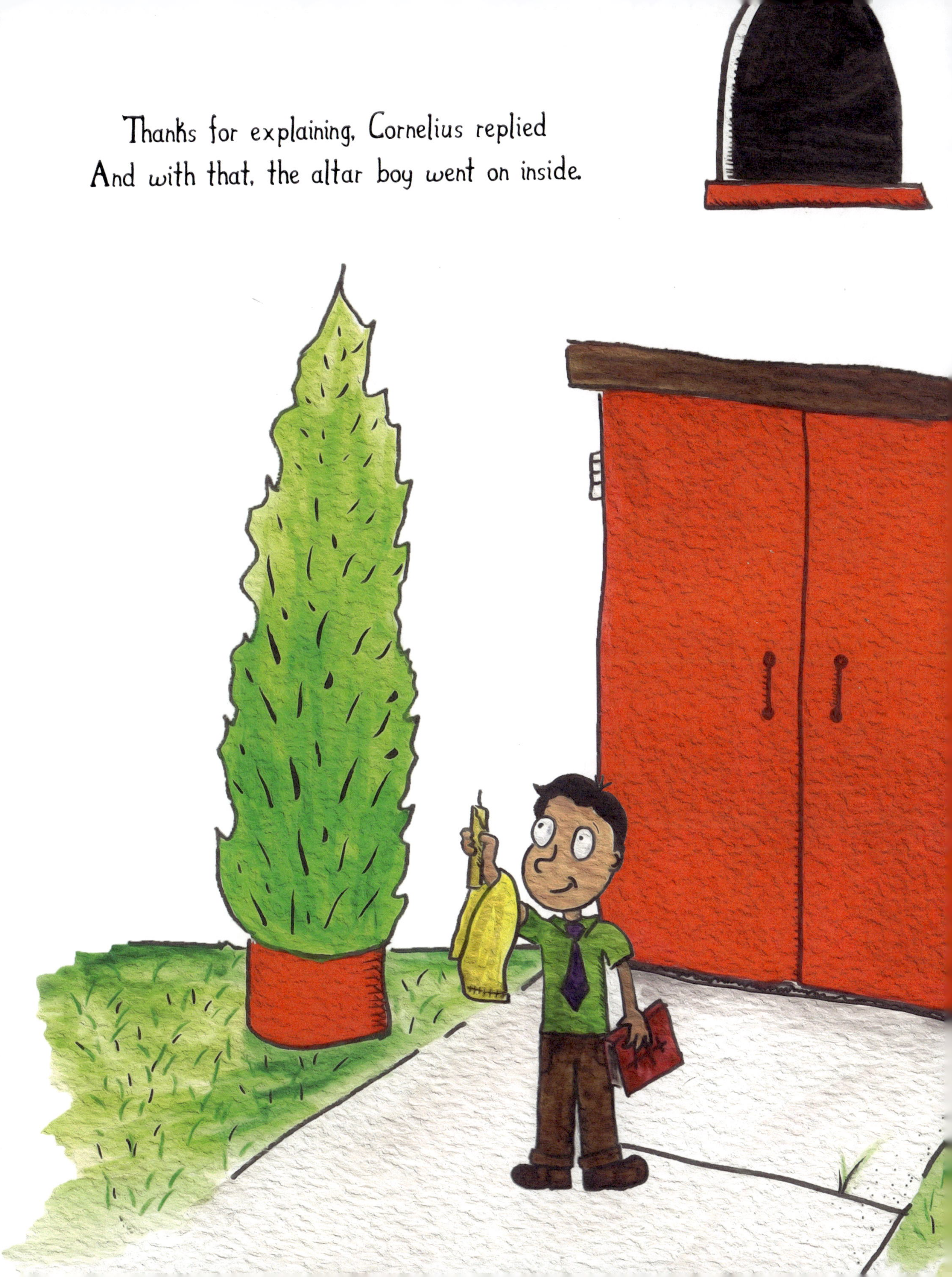

A few moments later, Cornelius discovered
A family approaching and with that, his wings fluttered.
WHO WHO ARE YOU? Cornelius asked
They stopped to answer before they passed.

We are a family, coming to pray.
We come here to worship God every Sunday.
We pray for peace, guidance, and blessings
And anything in our lives we feel needs addressing

We must be off before we are late.
Just as they turned, Cornelius said, 'Wait!
Can I come along and see the service you mentioned?
I promise I have the best of intentions.'
'Of course, all are welcome to join us in prayer.
Fly on down, and we'll save you a chair.'

So into the church Cornelius flew
And perched himself on the very front pew.
Cornelius heard the church bells ring,
And suddenly the chanter started to sing.

The liturgy was as lovely as can be.
There were so many things to smell, taste and see.
There were icons, candles, frankincense and myrrh.
God's love was all around, Cornelius was sure.

'That was the best' Cornelius said with a shriek.
'I can't wait to come back every week!'

Hieromartyr Cornelius the Centurion Troparion & Kontakion
Commemorated on September 13

Troparion in Tone 4

O Blessed Cornelius,
You were distinguished in works of righteousness.
You received the enlightenment of godliness,
And were a fellow-laborer with the Apostles,
For you shared in their work,
Preaching Christ's incarnation to all.
With them pray that all who honor your memory may be saved!

Kontakion in Tone 4

O Divinely minded Cornelius,
The Church, receiving you as a blessed first-fruit of the Gentiles,
Is enlightened by your holy life,
For you are a perfect seer of the Mysteries!

10% of the proceeds from this book will be donated to IOCC.

Made in the USA
Columbia, SC
06 November 2024